AF211666

LILI GREENE

CONFIDENCE GAME

The Essential Guide to Building Your Self-Confidence, Discover Helpful Tips to Increase Your Self-Confidence and Overcome Your Fears

Descrierea CIP a Bibliotecii Naţionale a României
LILI GREENE
  CONFIDENCE GAME. The Essential Guide to Building Your Self-Confidence, Discover Helpful Tips to Increase Your Self-Confidence and Overcome Your Fears / Lili Greene. – Bucharest: Editura My Ebook, 2020
  ISBN 978-606-983-583-8

LILI GREENE

CONFIDENCE GAME

**The Essential Guide to Building Your Self-Confidence,
Discover Helpful Tips to Increase Your Self-Confidence
and Overcome Your Fears**

My Ebook Publishing House
Bucharest, 2020

TABLE OF CONTENTS

Chapter 3

OVERCOMING YOUR LIMITING BELIEFS

Chapter 4

DAILY HABITS TO INCREASE
YOUR SELF ESTEEM

Chapter 5
MEDITATION FOR BUILDING
SELF-CONFIDENCE

INTRODUCTION

Everyone desires to be confident, yet very few have been able to develop it in all facets of their life. A lack of self-confidence can ultimately become the most significant hindrance to finding happiness, success, and fulfillment.

Unfortunately, too many people often are unable to see the effects low self-confidence has on their lives, blaming their failures on outside factors instead. They blame a tough dating scene for not finding the right partner.

They are desperate to find a better job but don't know where to start because the job market is so competitive. They wish they could follow their dreams but can't afford to fail. On the surface, these kinds of excuses seem like they are legitimate outside barriers, keeping us from finding true happiness.

However, when further examined, the justifications are all rooted in a lack of self-confidence. Past experiences have helped to develop your current mindset, and the past unknowingly plagues us as we grow into adults.

As adults, we often waste a ton of energy attempting to appear confident rather than developing real confidence. The importance society puts on outside appearances only reinforces the pressure to show false confidence.

This is just intensified with the popularity of reality television and social media. It has become the norm for our society to appear one way to everyone else, rather than focusing on making the changes internally that will allow us to alter our sense of self.

For example, many people will post photoshopped images to their social media profiles in the hope of garnering a ton of likes to help increase their shaky self-esteem. Hence, the façade of confidence trumps genuine, unwavering confidence.

So, many people are afraid to admit they lack confidence because it is seen as a personal weakness, while others wish they could have more confidence, but don't know where to start.

If you suffer from a lack of confidence, it will continue to hold you back, even if you become adept at faking it. The great news is, you can be one of the few people that learn how to build an undeniable, persistent, and genuine level of self-confidence that won't be affected by outside circumstances.

This guide will provide you with the tips and strategies to develop confidence in all areas of your life. You will also learn the ways you can develop a strong sense of self and unconditional self-love to get you through any challenges that you might face in your life.

The only difference between those who are successful and those who fail in life is the willingness to keep trying. Having confidence will provide you with the drive and the ability to work toward your goals without your limiting beliefs standing in your way.

CHAPTER 1

SELF-ESTEEM AND CONFIDENCE

Self-esteem and confidence are often used interchangeably to describe an individual's level of assurance, poise, self-respect, and security. While these two concepts are often related, they are not the same.

The main difference is that self-esteem is a constant, while confidence is something that fluctuates. It is vital that you are able to foster a strong sense of both. To do this, you must first understand the origins of both and how each can be affected and changed.

Confidence vs. Self Esteem

Confidence is a huge part of your overall well-being. Being confident will help with your career, relationships, self-image, interactions, and other aspects of your life.

It isn't uncommon for someone to be extremely confident in one area of their life, yet insecure in another. Being fully confident and comfortable with yourself in every situation is truly invaluable.

When you foster a strong sense of self-esteem, it will help you become more confident in all areas of your life. While confidence varies between circumstances, your self-esteem is a continuous part of your self-concept.

The higher your self-esteem, the more likely you will be comfortable facing a variety of situations in your life. Self-esteem is an underlying trait that directly affects how you perceive yourself in all circumstances. Self-esteem can be tricky because a lack of self-esteem will manifest in a variety of ways.

Generalized self-doubt is one way that low self-esteem can manifest. If you have low self-esteem, you may automatically assume that you won't be good at a task and will either give up or subconsciously sabotage yourself into failing. This is your self- concept trying to prove why it has low self-esteem.

If you repeatedly fail in a variety of circumstances, your subconscious says, "I told you this would happen." During every situation that you face, negative self-talk will rear its ugly head, telling you that you will fail, you'll look stupid, you'll embarrass yourself, and that others will harshly judge you. This negative self-talk is not accurate, but instead it originates from low self-esteem.

Humans are social creatures, which gives us the ability to pick up on indicators of high or low self-esteem. It is these indicators that often affect how we respond to one another. Those who have high self-esteem are more likely to get a job, create social connections, strike up conversations, etc.

It isn't that most people are looking to hurt those with low self- esteem intentionally, it is just a natural tendency for us to be attracted to those who exhibit confidence. We are all self-serving beings, innately trying to get ahead and when someone exudes confidence, it indicates they can help us get ahead in life.

The way in which we present ourselves can be a clear indication to those around us of our levels of confidence and self-esteem. Physical cues like slouching, talking sheepishly, or a constant downcast gaze, all indicate low self-esteem.

During conversations, expressing doubt, frequent verbalization for a need for reassurance, or indecisiveness, are also clear signs of low self-esteem. It is relatively easy to see these kinds of signs in young children and teenagers; however, many adults have learned to hide their insecurities.

Many of us have all adopted the fake-it-until-you-make-it attitude. Unfortunately, we are so focused on faking it that we never work toward fixing the underlying issues.

Another way in which low self-esteem manifests itself is a confidence-contingent outlook. It displays itself when a person relies entirely on their accomplishments to feed their self-esteem.

This is far harder to spot in ourselves and other people.

This kind of low self-esteem makes us have the need to succeed at everything so that we can feel good about ourselves.

They may also feel the urge to put others down to feel superior, which feeds their confidence temporarily. The critical factor in these cases is always contingent on outside factors and is always temporary.

It results in the continuing need to feed the self-esteem monster in an attempt to escape your true feelings. It is a vicious and draining cycle that is incompatible with peace, happiness, and real self-esteem.

If you know how to build your confidence in any situation, it will help you to develop your overall self-esteem. Confidence in separate situations is a necessary building block to retrain your mind to think more confidently.

As your confidence becomes more natural, self-esteem grows and becomes a part of your self-concept.

Thus, developing unwavering self-esteem, as well as knowing how to build confidence in specific situations effectively, are both essential components for success and well-being. So, how do you know if you lack confidence and have low self-esteem?

Here are five signs to determine if you need to work on your self-esteem and confidence.

Constant Indecisiveness

Being indecisive often is a sign that you don't trust yourself to make the right decision. Doubt and insecurities accompany this. Those who lack self-esteem are frequently riddled with self-doubt. Being indecisive in many situations may indicate low self-esteem, while having it in one or two situations may show a lack of confidence in those particular situations.

For example, if you are a new business owner, you may spend more time making decisions than a seasoned entrepreneur because you are frequently second-guessing yourself. As you learn and develop the appropriate skills, you'll increase your confidence. Thus, knowledge and experience will improve confidence in individual situations.

Focused on Outside Reassurance

Self-esteem comes from your self-assurance, which means that you are confident in all situations and aren't swayed by the opinions of others. One symptom of low self-esteem is often the frequent fluctuation in your mood based on the actions of others.

Again, if this only happens in a few situations, it merely indicates that you may have a lack of confidence in those areas. However, if it is a reoccurring theme across the board, it is an indication that you have low self-esteem.

For example, if you always need to be told that you look nice to feel good about your appearance, you likely have low confidence about your self-image. If you also need constant reassurance at work, in relationships, and during social interactions, this likely indicates that you have low self-esteem.

Hesitant to Speak Up

Being reluctant to voice your opinions is another sign you might have low self-esteem and lack confidence. It indicates an underlying doubt in what you have to say. It might mean that you are unsure if your opinion is valid, or you tell yourself that others are uninterested in what you have to say. You might fear that by speaking up, it will cause others to dislike you.

Having low confidence in a particular area may cause you to be hesitant about voicing your opinion because you may fear you are not knowledgeable enough in the field. If you are a new business owner and attend a networking event, you may not feel confident to share your thoughts with a 20-year veteran.

If you continuously fear speaking up, it is an indication that you are suffering from generalized low self-esteem. This might cause negative thoughts of doubt that ultimately prevent you from speaking up.

Inability to Take Criticism

Being focused on outside reassurances and a failure to take criticism often coincide in individuals with low self-esteem. When you need others' approval to feel good, then hearing criticism can be crushing. For these individuals, criticism is always taken as a personal attack on the ego rather than being looked at as feedback.

When you suffer from low self-esteem, the opinions of others are valued higher than your own self-worth, the criticism is taken as truth, instead of mere opinion. When you have high self-esteem, you use these criticisms as helpful feedback and are able to listen and discard it as an untrue opinion.

Give Up Easily

Self-doubt is a substantial cause and symptom of low self-esteem. Nobody is an expert when they try something for the first time, and it requires perseverance and overcoming obstacles before you can succeed at anything. Someone with wavering esteem can become easily defeated when they fail the first time.

While your confidence may feel shaky when you are first embarking on a new endeavor, with the appropriate level of self-esteem, you will be able to figure out how you can increase your confidence.

When you have low self-esteem, the shaky confidence can become overwhelming, causing you to give up, protecting yourself from the potential consequences and discomfort that may come with failure.

CHAPTER 2

HOW LIMITING BELIEFS CAN AFFECT

YOUR SELF-ESTEEM

Many people suffer from low self-esteem because of their limiting beliefs. Limiting beliefs are blind and unhealthy beliefs that stop and constrain you from achieving success in your life.

They are self-imposed prison walls that you have built to protect yourself from the fear of failure and humiliation. It is a fake label that you give yourself to lock yourself in a cocoon of safety.

The fear of stepping out of your comfort zone is so intense that you give up at the first hurdle that you come too. They ultimately stop you from going after your dreams. Our beliefs come from two sources, our experiences, and our influences.

Our Influences

From an early age, we are bombarded with opinions and information from our family, society, and the people closest to us. As we grow and form bonds with our classmates and others, our conscious and subconscious minds continue to absorb, filter, and process the information.

All of the interactions we have on a daily basis, influence us to think, act and believe a certain way. Most of this happens subconsciously.

If you grew up in a household that believed that family always comes first, the chances are that you have a close, well-connected family.

If you grew up around people who think the wealthy are lucky and get all the breaks, chances are you believe that your ability to become wealthy is a steep, and impossible climb. If you grew up in a family that believes in a good education, chances are you believe the same and now expect your kids to get a good education as well.

Our Experiences

We learn from every experience we encounter in life. Whether you consciously learn from the experience or not, doesn't matter. Regardless, our minds tend to form beliefs based on single, significant experiences or cumulative experiences of the same nature.

In fact, many of our limiting beliefs are as a result of our experiences. As a kid, if you performed poorly on a science test, you may begin to believe that science is a subject that you will never understand or succeed at.

If you've repeatedly been cheated on in your relationships, you may think that there are no good people in the world and that you'll never find love. If you've been passed up for a promotion at work, you may believe that you are unqualified to perform at a higher level.

Both our influences and our experiences work to determine what our beliefs are, and usually form during our childhood. As you begin to understand where your opinions come from, you can start to question them and ultimately change them.

How Limiting Beliefs Keep You from Living Your Life

Throughout your life, you've constructed beliefs in yourself and about the world, which can directly contribute to your way of life. What's surprising is that these beliefs can also have a physical effect on you.

The more reinforced the idea is, the more impact it can have on your body. Whether you know it or not, your body shows the physical and mental manifestation of limiting beliefs that surround your self-image.

Your limiting beliefs will cause you to feel like you will never be able to achieve a goal. This can result in decreasing your self- confidence, ultimately losing your self-esteem in the process.

As your self-esteem falters, you might start avoiding trying new things and going on new adventures because you will believe that the risks and dangers surrounding the experience to be destructive and even fatal.

This will result in you complaining to others and placing blame, without discovering the underlining source of trouble. This can result in you starting to lose the balance you want in life that is necessary to keep it healthy and running.

Limiting beliefs, tend to cause self-judgment that is unhealthy, leading you to feel the need to put up a mask and hide your true self from the world. The fear of not accepting who you are could result in you losing your self-identity without even realizing it.

The limiting beliefs that you hold can result in physical changes to the body as well. This includes continuous and persistent agitation, depression, anxiety, indecision, bad temper, queasiness, and other emotional problems.

This can change who you are and the way you talk to others. The tone of your speech changes and you will tend to be negative. It can cause you to always find ways to complain and blame others for your problems and failures.

Identifying Limiting Beliefs

The first step to overcoming your limiting beliefs is to identify them. Living with your limiting beliefs can lead you to live a mediocre life, one that is significantly different from your potential.

Unfortunately, limiting beliefs can be challenging to identify. Before you can begin to identify your limiting beliefs, you need to learn to keep track of your self-talk and become aware of the judgments that your subconscious is making.

By knowing how to keep track of the way you talk to yourself, you will be able to identify the limiting beliefs that run through your mind during conversations. Getting rid of the bias of your subconscious mind is another vital step in finding your limiting beliefs.

Some of the most common limiting beliefs include:

- I can't be my real, authentic self because I'll be judged.
- I can't fall in love because I'll get my heart broken.
- I can't ask for what I want because I'll get rejected.
- I can't trust people because they will eventually betray my trust.
- I can't pursue my dreams because I will most likely fail.
- I don't need to be successful, so I'm not going to even strive for success.
- It's too late to pursue my dreams.
- I'm nothing special because I've never accomplished anything exceptional.
- I don't deserve happiness because I'm not good enough.
- I hate the way I look, and there is nothing I can do to change.
- I am too weak and will never be able to find the strength to change.

CHAPTER 3

OVERCOMING YOUR LIMITING BELIEFS

Now that you have identified your limiting beliefs, it is time to work on overcoming them. Unfortunately, most people don't take the steps necessary to do this because they believe that by having an awareness of their limiting beliefs they will be able to think differently about their circumstances and lives.

While being aware of your limiting beliefs will encourage you to think about them differently, a significant number of your limiting beliefs have a ton of emotional investment behind them, which is ultimately where the problem lies.

Whenever you have a tremendous level of emotion invested in something, it can create a barrier to change. In order to make lasting change, you have to cut your ties. In fact, the deeper the conviction or belief, the more difficult you'll find the process and the longer it will take.

Lying at the cornerstone of any change that you want to make is the willingness to adapt to the changing conditions and circumstances that surround you. This is especially true when it comes to changing your limiting beliefs.

You Must Choose the Outcome You Desire

The very first step that you have to take to overcome your limiting beliefs is to choose the outcome that you desire. When you choose your desired outcome, you are able to gain more clarity about what it is in your life that you would like to change.

You have to ask yourself some tough questions and thoroughly consider your answers. You need to ask yourself:

- What goals would I like to achieve?

- What's currently preventing me from achieving my goals?

- What kind of person would I ideally like to become?

- What specifically do I want to change?

- What specific beliefs aren't working for me?

- What limiting beliefs are preventing me from achieving my desired outcomes?

Once you have become clear about the limiting beliefs that are holding you back, you can start the process of overcoming these limiting beliefs and increasing your self-esteem.

Questioning Your Limiting Beliefs

It is important to remember that your limiting beliefs are only as strong as those references that support them. Often, the limiting beliefs that you hold have a plethora of references that have helped to influence and shift your perspective on reality.

It is important to remember that these references started out as ideas, which turned into opinions, which later became your beliefs. If you want to change your limiting beliefs, you have to change your perspective and opinion about them. You can start to throw doubt on your limiting beliefs by asking yourself:

- Is the belief accurate?

- Have I always believed this? Why?

- Was there a time that I didn't believe this? Why?

- Is there evidence that can disprove this limiting belief?

- Are there times when this belief doesn't make rational sense?

- Will this belief help me get what I want? Will it help me reach my goals?

- What is the exact opposite way of thinking about this belief? How is this helpful?

These questions are designed to help you increase perspective and the possibilities of your situation. They are meant to encourage you to think outside the box, so you can begin to shift how you think about your limiting beliefs.

Consider the Consequences of Your Limiting Beliefs

Now that you have begun to throw some doubt on your limiting beliefs, it's time for you to consider the possible consequences of holding onto your limiting beliefs. To do this, you need to think long and hard about the following questions.

- What will the consequences be if I'm not able to make this change and eliminate this limiting belief?

- How will not making a change affect me emotionally? Physically? Financially? Spiritually? In my relationships?

- How will not making a change affect my life?

- Are there short-term consequences in not changing my life? What are they?

- Are there long-term consequences?

- What makes making this change now so essential?

The more pain that is associated with holding onto your limiting beliefs, the higher motivation you'll have to make positive changes in your life. That's why it is essential to move through each of these questions, one at a time to fully experience the pain. You want to feel the anger, think about the regrets, experience the guilt, and allow yourself to cry.

Choose a New Empowering Belief

In order to move forward after you've considered the consequences of holding onto your limiting beliefs, you need to choose a new empowering belief. It is vital that you make sure that this new belief is believable. If it isn't one that is believable, the chances are high that you will be unable to condition your psyche.

To unlock your new empowering belief, you need to consider the goal that you want to achieve, the person that you want to become, and the core values that you want to maintain. Once you have considered these, you need to ask yourself the following questions from a third person's perspective:

- What would this person likely believe while pursuing this goal?

- What would this person believe about themselves?

- What would this person believe about their goal?

- What's their attitude like? How do they think about the goal?

- How would they think about the obstacles they encounter along the journey?

Now, you need to take some time to consider the advantages of this new empowering belief and how it can improve your life and your circumstances. Ask yourself the following:

- What benefits can I expect from using this new belief?

- How will it help me reach my goals?

- How will it change my life for the better?

- How will it help in both the long-term and short-term?

- How will this new belief make me feel about myself?

- How will this new belief empower me moving forward?

- Why is this important?

The more reasons that you can find, the higher your motivation will be to break your old patterns of behavior and replace them with a new, empowering belief system.

Condition your New Belief

Now that you've committed yourself to changing your limiting beliefs to new empowering ones, the next step is to begin to condition your new beliefs into your psyche progressively.

One way to do this is through the process of visualization. Spend time every day visualizing yourself, in your imagination, using your new way of thinking in your day-to-day activities. Take particular note of the actions you take, the decisions you are making, how you talk to others, and how you talk to yourself.

Think about your newly formed attitude and how your new beliefs are going to help you manifest the life you want. You are in essence imagining a new you in your minds-eye.

Another process that you can use is the process of anchoring this new belief to condition it into your nervous system. This involves anchoring a sensation that is physical to your body that will allow it to automatically enable you to get into an optimal state of mind that corresponds to your new empowering belief.

It's not easy to overcome your limiting beliefs, but with a significant amount of work, introspection, and time, you'll be able to overcome the limiting beliefs that have been holding you back and build your self-confidence.

CHAPTER 4

DAILY HABITS TO INCREASE YOUR SELF ESTEEM

Now that you've have discovered how to identify and overcome your limiting beliefs, you can begin to rebuild your self-confidence by boosting your self-esteem. To do this, you have first to change your self-perception.

You need to change how you look at yourself and how you view yourself. Everybody has self-perception. Everyone has a mental picture in their minds of who they are, what they are capable of, and where they are going.

If you suffer from low self-confidence, you have a negative view of these things. You probably feel that you are not worth much of anything and that whatever you try will result in mediocrity or failure.

You have to work on your self-perception if you want to increase your self-esteem and build your self-confidence. To start the process of improving your self-esteem, you need to incorporate these daily habits into your life.

Change Your Self-Talk

Self-talk is merely the act of talking to yourself, either mentally or aloud. It is any thought that pops into your head in reaction to external stimuli. The way that you feel about situations depends on what you tell yourself.

If you think about the situation negatively, it will lead to negative emotions like irritation or anxiety. Thinking about the situation positively will lead to positive feelings like excitement or happiness.

When you are working on increasing your self-esteem, you become more aware of the constant self-talk that leads to negative feelings, and you can replace it with positive self-talk that encourages higher levels of self-esteem.

For example, if you are always telling yourself that you are fat every time you look in the mirror, you need to stop and replace these thoughts with words of encouragement.

In this example, you have trained yourself to look at areas of your body that make you insecure and reinforce your insecurity by saying "I'm fat."

If you teach yourself to look in the mirror and appreciate your body or focus on an area that you feel good about, over time, this will shift your self-image and confidence.

Practice Affirmations

Affirmations are simple, positive statements that you say about yourself to change negative thinking patterns. You can say a set of affirmations every day or use them to replace negative self-talk. Affirmations help to improve self-esteem by implanting new beliefs to replace beliefs that cause low self-esteem.

When you are trying to change your automatic thoughts and negative self-talk, it is helpful to have a set of affirmations to use in place of the old, negative thinking patterns that you have developed. With enough repetition, affirmations will become implanted into your subconscious mind.

Stop Comparisons

You have to recognize you are unique. You also have to realize that you never get the full story and that everyone puts on a front in an attempt to disguise their insecurities.

When you compare yourself to others, you are merely comparing yourself to the façade others are presenting to the world.

Everyone has thoughts, doubts, insecurities, judgments and other inner battles that they deal with in their minds.

You also need to stop using comparisons to make yourself feel good about yourself. It is tempting to do in an effort to feed your own ego, but it turns into a vicious cycle.

When you use comparisons to make yourself feel better, your brain will automatically use it to make you feel worse. The only way to escape this is to cut yourself off from making comparisons between yourself and others.

Eliminate Judgment

Judgment is one of the most destructive and least productive habits you can develop. Unfortunately, few live a life that is free form judgmental thoughts. Judgment and true confidence are incompatible. One can never experience genuine peace while holding onto judgments.

Judgment becomes habitual in us; we naturally do it without even realizing it. We judge ourselves as a form of punishment for not being perfect, and we judge others in an attempt to make ourselves feel better.

People who are truly happy with themselves do not feel the urge to judge others or themselves.

The first step on the path to this kind of freedom is accepting that there is nothing perfect in the universe.

You need to learn to take yourself as you are and accept others in the same way. Everyone came into this world with different personalities, have had various experiences that have shaped us and we all continue to face challenges. Judging anyone is unfair.

Incorporate Self-Care

Neglecting your own needs can contribute to low self-esteem, as well as being a symptom of low self-esteem. Self-care is merely doing something because it makes you happy.

It can be as simple as relaxing in a bubble bath, enjoying a massage, or taking a walk by yourself. Self-care is often looked at as selfishness. People often feel guilty for spending time on themselves because they think that it is taking away the happiness of others.

The first step to change this is to recognize you are worthy of time and attention and release any thoughts that cause guilt. Next, you need to think of one thing that you can add in on a regular basis that is 100 percent for you.

Tell your loved ones that you are doing it and be as committed to yourself as you have been to everyone else.

Let go of Perfectionism

Perfectionism is often a cover-up for insecurity. It is also the number one enemy of confidence. Perfectionism comes from an underlying belief that you must be perfect to deserve love and acceptance from yourself and others.

It indicates that an individual places his or her self-worth on accomplishments and defines his or her self-concept based on actions. This mindset leads to drastic fluctuations in mood and confidence and immense pressure to always get it right.

You need to let go of your perfectionistic tendencies. You have to foster an unconditional love and acceptance for yourself and know you are separate from your actions and accomplishments. The more willing you are to accept yourself when you make mistakes, the higher your self-esteem will become.

Celebrate Daily Victories

It can become overwhelming when we are trying to change any aspect of our lives. Changes take time, and it can only happen with daily actions.

There have been plenty of people who have been able to overcome shyness and develop a healthy self-esteem, but it wasn't accomplished overnight. To stay motivated on your path to increasing your self-esteem and building your confidence, you have to recognize and celebrate the small victories.

Celebrating small victories when working toward any goal will also help to build your confidence. You deserve credit and have to be willing to give yourself recognition. If you are always focusing on how far away you are from reaching your end goal, your journey may turn into a struggle, filled with doubt and disappointment.

Instead, celebrate the small accomplishments along the journey and become filled with the encouragement and the energy to continue.

Practice Gratitude

Individuals with low self-esteem tend to focus on the negative experiences and lack in their lives. It is easy to focus on what you want but don't have, and it takes an effort to change this outlook.

Expressing appreciation and gratitude for everything in your life will transform your perspective during each moment and eventually alter your perceptions of yourself and the world.

When practicing gratitude, be thankful for the blessings in your life, and who you are as a person. Take a moment to list three unique things that you appreciate in yourself and three things that you are grateful for in your life. Try to incorporate a practice of gratitude for yourself and the world on a daily basis and see the impact it has on your overall self-esteem.

Set Realistic Expectations

The quickest way to kill your confidence is to set high expectations for yourself. Setting goals and working toward them can help you build your confidence. However, if you set unrealistic standards, you will only end up feeling defeated.

If you have something that you want to work toward, come up with a realistic goal that you can work on today. Keep your goals small and attainable and be sure to celebrate each small victory.

CHAPTER 5

MEDITATION FOR BUILDING SELF- CONFIDENCE

Because self-esteem and confidence stem from thinking patterns, developing skills to both calm the mind and manipulate your belief system will promote a centered and confident internal state.

The following four meditation techniques will help you to clear your mind and focus on visualizing confidence. They will help you to implant new belief systems into your subconscious and help you to think and act confidently.

Mindful Meditation

Mindfulness meditation is the practice of clearing your mind and focusing on nothing but the here and now without trying to change anything and without judgment. Engaging in this practice every day will allow you to control your stress and anxiety.

The more you work on it, the stronger your mindfulness power and endurance will become. When you are first starting a routine of mindfulness meditation, it is best to start with shorter amounts of time and increase your duration slowly.

You also want to practice your meditation at the same time each day. The more you practice on a regular, consistent basis, the better the results.

Here are the steps to begin your daily practice of mindfulness meditation.

Step 1: Find a comfortable place to either sit up or lie straight. Sitting is often better because you are less likely to fall asleep.

Step 2: Set a timer. When you are first starting with your practice, it is better to keep your session around ten minutes. However, you can certainly increase this time if you feel you are able to sustain a more extended session.

Step 3: Begin taking calm breaths. Paying attention to how your breath feels going in your nose, down your lungs, and back out your nose. Pay attention to how your stomach or chest rises and falls with each breath.

It is essential that you don't change your breathing or make any judgments. Breathe normally and merely focus on your breath and body.

Step 4: Next, you want to do a body scan. Start at the top of your head. Notice how it feels. Next, move down to your face. What do the back of your eyelids look like? How do your lips, nose, and chin feel? Continue this process as you move down your entire body.

Pay attention to feeling and temperature. Notice if there is any tightness or tension in your body, but don't try to change or fix any of the sensations. This process is about you merely noticing feelings and moving on.

Step 5: After you've completed the body scan, pay attention to the noises around you. First, notice the sounds of your body. Are you able to hear your breathing? Focus on just that sound. Next, focus on the sounds that are in the room.

What noises are in the space? Then move onto the noises outside the space. What noises can you hear? Finally, focus your attention on the noises outside your living space. Can you hear anything?

Step 6: Finally, pay attention to how it feels to be in the moment. Let the thoughts that float into your mind float out again. Don't judge yourself for falling out of a mindfulness state and don't judge the thoughts that enter your mind. Don't attach any emotions to anything. Simply focus on each sensation that you feel.

Step 7: If you find one of the techniques works better for you, carry out the rest of your session using that technique, if not, just "be" until your timer rings.

Breathing Meditation

This technique helps to both focus and calm the mind, while physically relaxing the body. As with mindfulness meditation, you'll want to set a timer so that you can focus exclusively on your breathing without having to worry about the time.

Any time you feel overwhelmed, this technique can be extremely beneficial. It is effortless to practice because you can do it anywhere.

To prepare yourself for this meditation practice, you can either lie down or sit in a chair with your eyes open or closed. For a more profound relaxation, it is recommended that you sit or lie in a quiet space with your eyes closed.

Take deep inhales into your stomach, and fully exhale until you empty all the air from your lungs, making sure that each breath is rhythmic and consistent.

During this technique, inhale deeply until your belly rises and exhale fully as your stomach collapses and pulls in. The length of each breath isn't nearly as important as the consistency throughout your session.

Visualization

This kind of meditation practice will allow you to envision yourself acting confidently in all situations. You can use visualization before any significant event that causes you anxiety or use it daily to help you build your confidence over time. Follow the steps below to begin practicing visualization.

Step 1: Start your session with a few rounds of calm and controlled breathing. Only focus on your breath until both your body and mind become relaxed.

Step 2: Once you are in a relaxed state, say the following mantra: "I am confident" and feel confidence take over your entire being.

Step 3: In your mind, envision a clear, protective bubble forming around you. This is a shield where nothing negative can enter.

Imagine that you are safe, secure, and radiating self-esteem in the bubble.

Step 4: Imagine your day ahead. Imagine that you are confidently approaching every situation, protected by this bubble of self- esteem. You walk with your head held high, interact with others confidently, speak assertively, and never doubt yourself.

Step 5: As you imagine each situation, continue to allow yourself to be filled with confidence. You visualize that you always know exactly what to say. Others see you as a successful and confident person. You are overflowing with happiness, positivity, and assurance.

Step 6: Continue this process until you have gone through every upcoming event. End the meditation session by affirming, "I will live this day radiating self-esteem and at peace with myself in all situations."

Anchoring

Anchoring is a Neuro-Linguistic Programming technique that is used to induce a frame of mind or emotion. It is a conditioning that forms when a person evokes a feeling and pairs it with a gesture or touch of some kind.

To practice this technique, you need to get into a meditative state. Use mindfulness, breathing, or any combination to start. Then, you want to think of an emotion that you want to condition; it can be success, confidence, relaxation, or happiness. Now, picture a time in your life when you experienced the desired emotion.

If you aspire to feel confident, think of a time in your past when you experienced confidence. Perhaps, it was when you received the top grade in a class, or when your high school football team won the state championship.

Picture in your mind that moment and experience the emotions as if they are currently happening. While feeling the emotion, hold your index finger and thumb together. Relax for a few seconds, then reimagine the experience with a heightened state of feeling and bring your thumb and index finger together again.

Repeat this process three to five times. By repeating this exercise daily, when you put your thumb and index finger together, eventually you'll experience the same emotion, no matter the circumstance.

You can use this technique to recondition your thinking. For example, if you anchor a feeling of confidence, anytime you experience feelings of overwhelm or doubt, you can use this anchor to stimulate a positive, confident state.

Anchoring can also be used with other visualization techniques as well. For instance, once you have set your anchor, you can visualize being confident in your current or future pursuits.

Engage the anchor by merely placing your index finger and thumb together and experience the emotional response of confidence, making your visualization more real.

CONCLUSION

You now have a plethora of techniques that can help you to improve your self-esteem and build your confidence. While they are easy to read about, if you don't take action, the information you've gathered will be meaningless.

The effort you make in overcoming your limiting beliefs and increasing your confidence will set you apart from everyone else who desires more but has yet to take the necessary steps to move forward.

While you may feel frightened by this action, it is important to remember that all fear that you experience is in your mind. You can overcome it. It just takes a little push of your willpower to get the ball moving.

Take some time to think about which simple confidence hacks you can begin to implement today. It is often far easier to pick one technique and master it before moving on to the next.

Confidence, or lack of confidence in your case, doesn't develop overnight, so be patient with the process. Whatever path you choose to take, you are one step closer to reaching your ultimate goal of boosting your self-esteem and building your confidence, so you can finally begin living the life you've always dreamed.

Printed by Libri Plureos GmbH in Hamburg, Germany